*322 Words*

# CHILDREN'S ILLUSTRATED DICTIONARY

Published by AM Productions
Ottawa, Canada
(613) 745-3098

Text and Design by Astrid Anand
Illustrations by Glick-Art


Printed in Canada

This ***Children's Illustrated Dictionary*** will quickly help beginning readers to recognize and understand the meaning of over 300 basic English words from the letters A through Z.

Each word is clearly defined and then used in one or more sample sentences. Lively illustrations in full color enhance the text. Each word has its own, easily recalled image.

The twenty-six letters of the English alphabet are printed in sequence, in capitals and lower case, at the top of each page. Young children will thereby learn what a dictionary is and how to use it.

Although designed for young children, this ***Children's Illustrated Dictionary*** will appeal to parents, older siblings and teachers as well.

# Aa

**accident**

something unlucky that happens by chance. Sam had an **accident** — he slipped on a banana peel and fell.

---

**accordion**

a box-shaped musical instrument. He squeezes the **accordion** while pressing on the keys and buttons.

---

**acrobat**

someone who performs difficult jumping and balancing acts. An **acrobat** gets a lot of applause.

---

**adult**

a fullly grown person or animal. I was a child, then a teenager and now I am an **adult**. **Adults** take care of their young.

---

**air**

what everybody breathes. You take a deep breath of fresh, cool **air**. On windy days the **air** moves fast and blows things around.

---

**airplane**

a flying machine with wings and engines. An **airplane** flies over land and sea to distant places.

---

**alarm clock**

a clock with a buzzer or a bell to wake you up. I keep an **alarm clock** beside my bed to wake me up in the morning.

# Aa

**ambulance** a van for taking hurt or sick people to a hospital. I hear the siren of an **ambulance**.

---

**ant**

a tiny insect that lives in large groups. This **ant** is drawn much larger than life. The **ant** is waving one of its six legs.

---

**antler** the branched horn on the head of a deer. Male deer shed and regrow their **antlers** every year.

---

**ape**

an animal like a large monkey with no tail, with long arms and a big brain. The smart chimpanzee is an **ape**. Gorillas are **apes**.

---

**apple** a hard, round fruit that grows on trees. I eat a crisp, red **apple**. This green **apple** tastes as sweet as the red or yellow one.

---

**armchair**

a comfortable, padded chair with high sides for resting your arms. Kelly sits in an **armchair** to relax.

---

**astronaut** a person who travels in space. An **astronaut** leaves Earth in a space ship and soon lands on the Moon.

# Bb

**baby**

a very young child. This is a picture of me when I was a **baby**. All three **babies** are sleeping in one big crib.

---

**balloon**

a bag that can be filled with air or hot gas. A party **balloon** meets a hot-air **balloon** floating in the sky.

---

**bank**

a safe place to keep your money. This kind of **bank** has a slot in the top for saving coins. We call it a *piggy* **bank**.

---

**barn**

a big farm building for animals and for storing things. The farmer stores hay in his **barn**. Cows sleep in the **barn**.

---

**basket**

a container, for holding or carrying things, made of straw. She carries home a **basket** full of strawberries.

---

**bat**

a small animal with large ears, a furry body and leathery wings. Most **bats** sleep by day and fly around at night.

---

**bathtub**

a large basin for holding water, to wash yourself in. He takes a bubble bath in the **bathtub**.

# Bb

**bear** a large animal with thick fur, sharp claws and a pointed snout. This trained **bear** works in the circus.

---

**beaver**

a furry animal with a paddle-tail, sharp teeth and webbed hind feet. The **beaver** is a strong swimmer.

---

**bed** a piece of furniture on which you sleep. The mattress on the **bed** feels lumpy. At what time do you go to **bed**?

---

**bee**

a flying insect that can make honey. **Bees** are buzzing in the flowers. An angry **bee** can sting you.

---

**bell** a hollow, metal object that rings when struck. On Christmas Eve the church **bells** ring at midnight.

---

**bicycle**

a two-wheeled vehicle that you can ride. You pedal a **bicycle** with your feet and steer it with your hands.

---

**bird** an animal with feathers and wings. Most **birds** can fly. An ostrich is a **bird** that runs fast, but cannot fly.

**blanket**

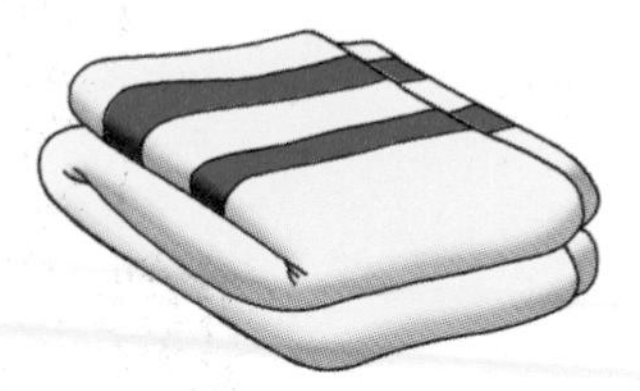

a thick cover for a bed. You sleep under a **blanket** to keep yourself warm in bed.

---

**boat**

something that floats, used for taking people or things over water. A motor **boat** is racing across the lake.

---

**book**

a set of printed pages fastened together inside a cover. This is a **book** with words and pictures.

---

**bottle**

a plastic or glass container with a narrow neck, for holding liquids. I drink a small **bottle** of lemonade.

---

**boy**

a male child. Alan, Brian and Charles are English names for **boys**. The **boy** with the new bicycle has a Spanish name – José.

---

**branch**

a part of a tree, growing from its trunk. Flowers grow on the **branches** of some trees. The **branch** snapped in the wind.

---

**bread**

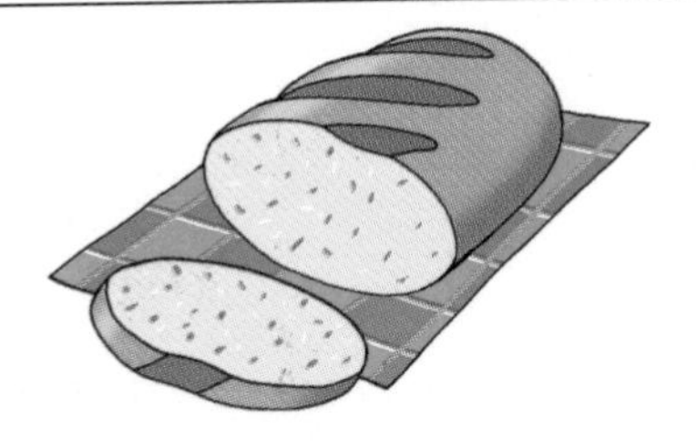

food, baked in an oven, made of flour, water and often yeast. You go to the bakery to buy a fresh loaf of **bread**.

# Bb

**bridge** a structure built for people and vehicles to cross a river, road or railway. A new stone **bridge** spans the Little River.

---

**brush**

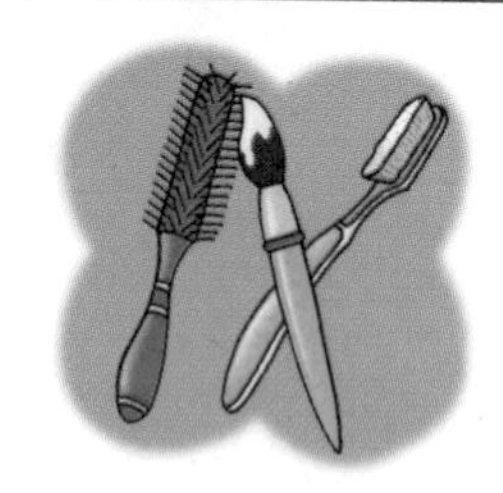

an object with short, stiff hairs attached to a handle. You use all kinds of **brushes**: a *hair***brush**, a *tooth***brush**, a *paint* **brush**.

---

**buckle** a clip to fasten the ends of a belt or strap. This leather belt has a fancy gold **buckle**.

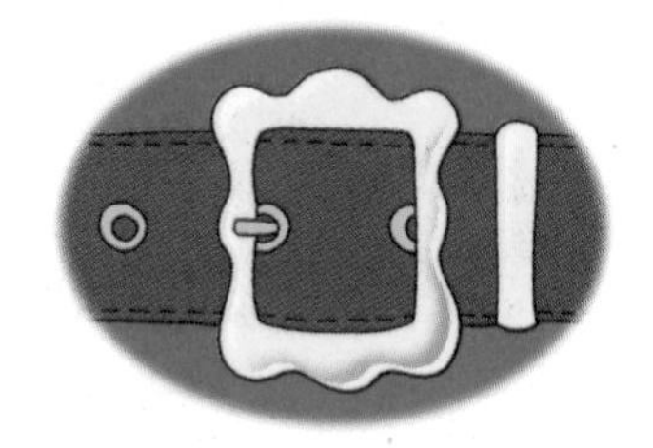

---

**bulldozer**

a heavy machine for moving rocks and earth. The road builders use **bulldozers** to clear the land.

---

**bunch** some things that are bundled together or grow together. I buy a **bunch** of flowers. Bananas grow in **bunches**.

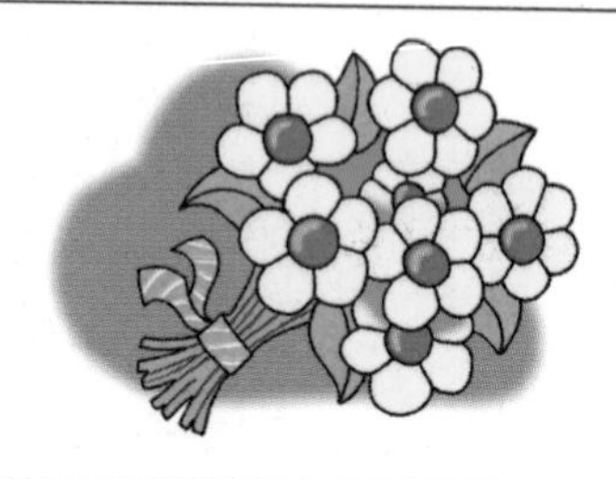

---

**bus**

a large, road vehicle with rows of seats for many passengers. Two city **buses** stop to let the yellow school **bus** pass.

---

**butterfly** a flying insect with large, colorful wings. A **butterfly** starts life as a creeping, crawling caterpillar.

**camera**

an instrument for taking photographs. Is the **camera** loaded with film? Just aim your **camera** and snap a picture.

---

**candle**

a stick of wax with a string through the middle. A burning **candle** gives light. Please light the **candles** on my cake.

---

**canoe**

a light, narrow boat that comes to a point at both ends. She paddles her **canoe** across the river.

---

**car**

a vehicle with an engine and four wheels for carrying a driver and a few passengers. This **car** runs on gasoline.

---

**castle**

a house and fortress with towers and high walls built in the Middle Ages. Knights in armor defended their lord and lady's **castle**.

---

**cat**

a furry animal with whiskers that you can keep as a pet. **Cats** can see in the dark. Our **cat** is not afraid of dogs.

---

**celery**

a green vegetable with long, crisp stalks and leafy tops. Molly munches on sticks of **celery**, instead of candy.

# Cc

**chair** a piece of furniture for one person to sit on. A **chair** has four legs and a back you can lean against.

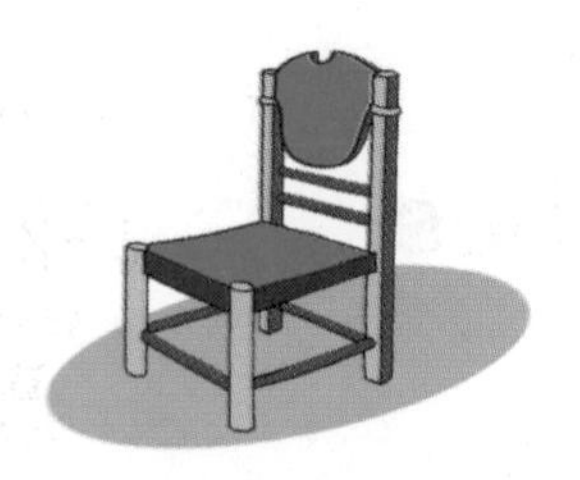

---

**chameleon**

a lizard that changes color to match its surroundings. This **chameleon** has turned leaf-green.

---

**cherry** a small, round, red fruit with a stone inside. **Cherries** grow on trees. The juice of a **cherry** is red and sweet.

---

**chicken**

a young farm bird, kept for its meat and eggs. The **chicken** lays an egg. These corn-fed **chickens** are plump.

---

**circus** a traveling show with trained animals, acrobats and clowns. The teacher is taking her class to see the **circus**.

---

**clock**

an instrument that shows us the time. This **clock** has hands to point to the time. Other **clocks** just display the changing time.

---

**clog** a heavy, wooden shoe. Mother wears a pair of **clogs** to work in the garden. A tulip design is painted on each **clog**.

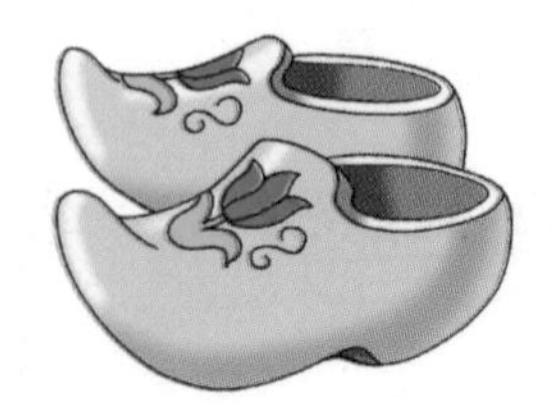

**clothes**

things you wear to cover your body. When it's too cold for shorts, you put on warmer **clothes** to go out.

---

**cloud**

a mass of water droplets floating in the sky. Rain falls from **clouds**. The sun peeks out from behind a **cloud**.

---

**clown**

a performer who makes people laugh. A **clown** wears funny clothes and make-up and does silly things.

---

**coach**

a vehicle with seats inside that is pulled by horses. The Queen of England still rides in a golden **coach**.

---

**coat**

a piece of clothing with long sleeves to wear outdoors, over other clothes. In winter she wears a **coat** with a hood.

---

**compass**

an instrument with a needle that always points north. We used a **compass** to find our way home.

---

**computer**

a machine that stores, organizes and gives information. Even as I type, the **computer** underlines my mistakes.

# Cc

**cow** a farm animal kept for its milk. A **cow** is the female of the bull family. Some **cows** have horns.

---

**crab**

a sea animal with a hard shell, eight legs and two large, front claws. A **crab** will wave one claw to signal to his mate.

---

**crib** a baby's bed with high sides. The high sides of a **crib** stop the baby from rolling out of bed.

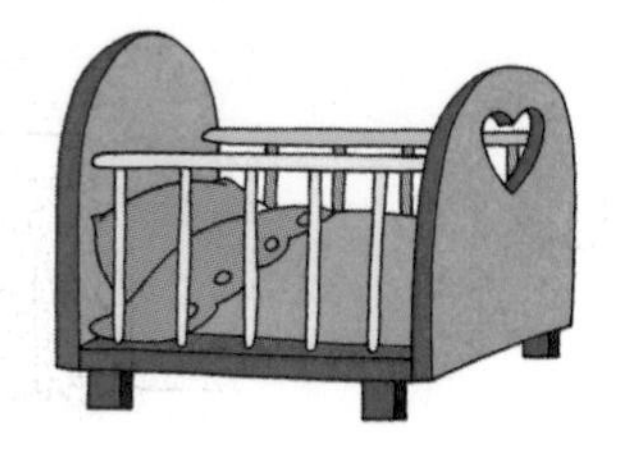

---

**crown**

a headdress of gold worn by a king or queen on special occasions. The queen sits on a throne and wears a jewelled **crown**.

---

**cup** a small bowl with a handle from which you can drink. A hot **cup** of tea sits on a saucer. The **cup's** handle stays cool.

---

**curtain**

a piece of material that hangs across a window or theatre stage. The **curtains** covering the window are drawn back.

---

**cutlery** utensils used at the table to eat our food. Knives, forks and spoons are **cutlery**. We keep the **cutlery** in a kitchen drawer.

# Dd

**daffodil**

a yellow flower that grows from a bulb planted in the soil. The **daffodil** is a spring time flower.

---

**dart**

a small arrow that you throw at a round target. You use a **dart** to score points in the game of **darts**.

---

**desk**

a kind of table at which you sit to read and write. The teacher sits down at her **desk** to correct our homework.
.

---

**dessert**

sweet food eaten at the end of a meal. The waiter cleared away our plates and served ice cream for **dessert**.

---

**dice**

small cubes with black dots, from one to six, for playing games. You roll two **dice** when playing 'Snakes and Ladders'.

---

**dinosaur**

a large animal that lived millions of years ago. The nickname for this firece **dinosaur** is T-Rex.

---

**doctor**

a person who is trained to make sick and injured people well again. Stella is a **doctor** at the children's hospital.

# Dd

**dog**

an animal that barks, that you can keep as a pet. What kind of **dog** is that? The **dogs** chase each other in the park.

---

**doll**

a toy in the shape of a person or a baby. This **doll** has curly hair. Martha collects **dolls** from around the world.

---

**dolphin**

a warm-blooded animal that lives in fresh and salt water. A **dolphin** can be taught to perform clever tricks.

---

**donkey**

an animal with long, pointed ears that looks like a horse. A **donkey** can carry heavy loads on its back.

---

**dragon**

a winged, fire-breathing creature in stories and legends. Only a super hero can slay the evil **dragon**.

---

**drum**

a hollow musical instrument that you strike. You beat a **drum** with your hands or with sticks.

---

**duck**

a water bird with a flat beak and webbed feet. A **duck** paddles its feet to swim. Wild **ducks** fly south.

**eagle**

a big bird that hunts other animals for its food. An **eagle** has sharp claws, a hooked beak and far-seeing eyes.

---

**earth**

the planet on which we live, and the soil in which plants grow. **Earth** is a planet that supports all kinds of life.

---

**egg**

an oval object with a shell, made by a hen. We eat cooked **eggs**. A painted Easter **egg** tells us, "Spring is here!"

---

**elbow**

the place in the middle of your arm where it bends. Your arm hinges at the **elbow**. The **elbow** joint works like a hinge.

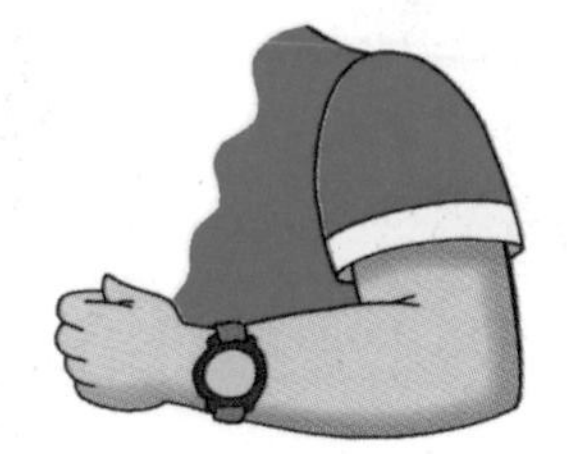

---

**elephant**

a large animal with thick gray skin, big ears and a long trunk. An **elephant** uses its trunk like an arm and hand.

---

**evergreen**

a tree that has green leaves all year round. The leaves of an **evergreen** are often needle-thin in shape.

---

**eye**

the part of the body used for seeing. Human **eyes** need light to see. If he winks one **eye**, then I know it's a joke.

# Ff

**face** the front of your head. You recognize people by their **faces**. Her mood changed and the frown on her **face** turned into a smile.

---

**factory**

a building where machines are used to make things. This **factory** makes cars. Many **factories** have tall smoke stacks.

---

**farm** land and the buildings on it where crops are grown and animals are raised for food. This **farm** is miles away from the city.

---

**fence**

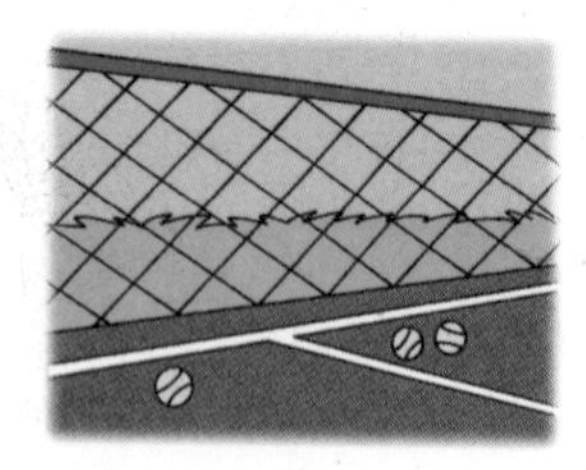

a barrier that closes off an area and blocks the way. The playground is enclosed by a high, wire **fence**.

---

**fire** the heat, light and flames produced when something is burning. The **fire** burning in the **fire***place* keeps the room warm.

---

**fish**

an animal with scales and fins that lives and breathes under water. A **fish** uses its tail to move through the water.

---

**flag** a piece of colored cloth used as a sign or a symbol. He waves a red **flag** to stop the train. Every country has a **flag** of its own.

**flamingo**

a large, long-legged bird with pink feathers. A **flamingo** wades in the water. I saw **flamingoes** in Florida.

---

**flower**

the part of a plant that produces seeds. The seeds of this **flower** can be eaten, or pressed to give us *sun***flower** oil.

---

**food**

the things you eat that help you to grow and be healthy. We eat **food** everyday. Farmers and ranchers grow our **food**.

---

**fossil**

plant or animal remains that are ages old and rock hard. These **fossils** are many millions of years old.

---

**fountain**

water that shoots out of a spout up into the air and falls down again. There is a **fountain** in the park.

---

**friend**

a person you like who also likes you. Saul and Clara are best **friends**. Best **friends** like to do things together.

---

**frog**

a small animal that lives both on land and in water. With long back legs and webbed feet, a **frog** leaps and swims.

# Gg

**galaxy** a huge group of stars and planets. Our sun is one of billions of stars in a **galaxy** called the Milky Way.

---

**gate**

a kind of door in a wall or a fence. We lock the **gate** to keep the dog inside the yard. The **gate** swings on hinges.

---

**genie** an imaginary being with magical powers. "Your wish is my command," said the **genie** of the magic lamp to Aladdin.

---

**ghost**

the empty shape of a dead person that some people imagine they can see. Is that tower really haunted by a **ghost**?

---

**giant** a big, scary person in fairy tales. A wicked **giant** is the villain in a story about Jack and the magic beanstalk.

---

**gift**

something that is given; a present. They come to the birthday party bringing **gifts**. This beautifully wrapped **gift** is for you.

---

**giraffe** a very tall animal with a very long neck and dark patches on its skin. **Giraffes** live in Africa. I saw a **giraffe** at the zoo.

**girl**

a female child. Laura, Karen and Jane are English names for **girls**. A **girl** will grow up to be a woman.

---

**glasses**

lenses set in a frame that you wear in front of your eyes to see better. This pair of **glasses** has a red frame.

---

**globe**

an object shaped like a ball. This is a **globe** with a map of the whole world on it. You can spin the **globe** around.

---

**glove**

a covering for the hand with four fingers and a thumb. You wear a pair of **gloves** to warm up or protect your hands.

---

**glue**

a thick liquid or paste used to stick things together. Wallpaper sticks to the wall with **glue**. A drop of **glue** can fix a broken toy.

---

**goblin**

a small and nasty creature in fairy tales. The stories tell us that a **goblin** likes to play mean tricks on people.

---

**goose**

a big bird with a long neck and webbed feet. A farmyard **goose** is not used to flying. Wild **geese** fly south in winter.

# Gg

**gorilla** the largest of the apes. **Gorillas** live on the ground in the forests of Africa. The **gorilla** dines on fruits and leaves.

---

**grape**

a juicy, green or purple fruit that grows in bunches on a vine. I pick a **grape** from a bunch of **grapes** and I eat it.

---

**graph** a diagram to show changes in a quantity or value. This **graph** diagrams the weather for June.

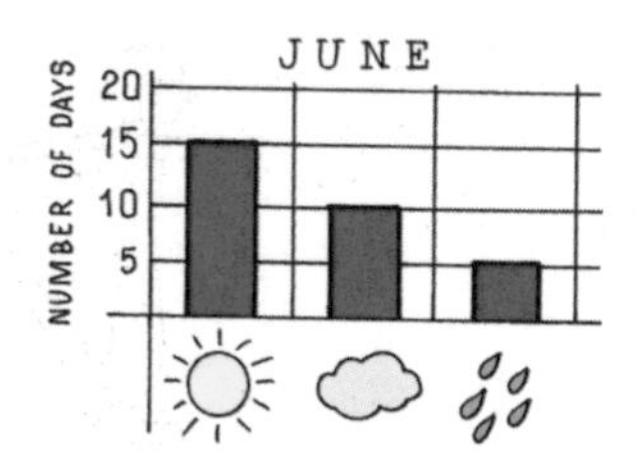


---

**grass**

a plant with thin, green leaves. **Grass** grows in fields and on lawns. I watch a ladybug climb up a blade of **grass**.

---

**grasshopper** a small, high-jumping insect. A **grasshopper** chirps by rubbing one leg against a wing.

---

**greenhouse**

a glass building where plants are grown. A **greenhouse** traps the heat of the sun.

---

**guitar** a musical instrument with strings that you pluck. She plays pop, rock and the blues on an electric **guitar**.

# Hh

**haircut**

the cutting of someone's hair, or, the way it is cut. Do not try to give yourself a **haircut**!

---

**hammer**

a heavy tool used for hitting nails. The carpenter uses a **hammer** to nail two pieces of wood together.

---

**harp**

a musical instrument with strings that you pluck with your fingers. Large or small, a **harp** is shaped like a triangle.

---

**hat**

something you wear to cover your head. Different **hats** can either cool or warm your head. Sue wears a cowboy's **hat**.

---

**heart**

the body part that pumps the blood around inside you, or, its curved shape. She drew musical notes in the shape of a **heart**.

---

**helicopter**

an aircraft with spinning blades on its roof. A **helicopter** takes off by rising straight into the air.

---

**helmet**

a hard hat that protects your head from injury. Knights in armor wore **helmets**. I wear a bicycle **helmet**.

# Hh

**herb** a plant used in making medicines and in cooking. Mint is a **herb** used for making tea and flavoring medicines and candy.

---

**highway**

a main road that connects cities and towns. A **highway** allows people to drive a long way at high speeds.

---

**hill** higher ground. You need special skills to climb a mountain, but not to climb a **hill**. They march up the **hill** in single file.

---

**hole**

an opening or a gap in something. They played eighteen **holes** of golf. That **hole** in the road goes down to the city sewers.

---

**horse** a four-legged animal with hooves, a tail and a long mane. The cowboys saddle their **horses**. Sam rides a gentle **horse**.

---

**hospital**

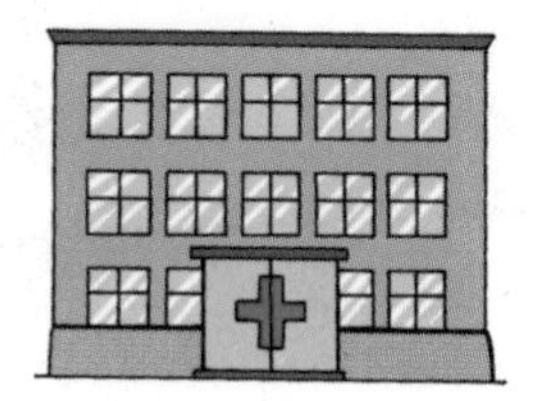

a building with beds and equipment where doctors and nurses take care of sick and injured people. I visit Amy in the **hospital**.

---

**house** a building where people live together, often as a family. They moved to a new **house** in the suburbs. My **house** has a tiny backyard.

**ice**

frozen water. A huge mass of **ice** floating in the sea is an **ice***berg*. How quickly a piece of **ice** melts in your warm hand!

---

**infant**

a newborn baby. The mother wraps her **infant** in a little blanket. A lot of loving care is what an **infant** needs.

---

**initial**

the first letters of someone's name. The towel with the **initials** G.A.W. belongs to George Allen Wheeler.

---

**insect**

a small creature with six little legs. Ladybugs and butterflies are flying **insects**. An ant is a crawling **insect**.

---

**iron**

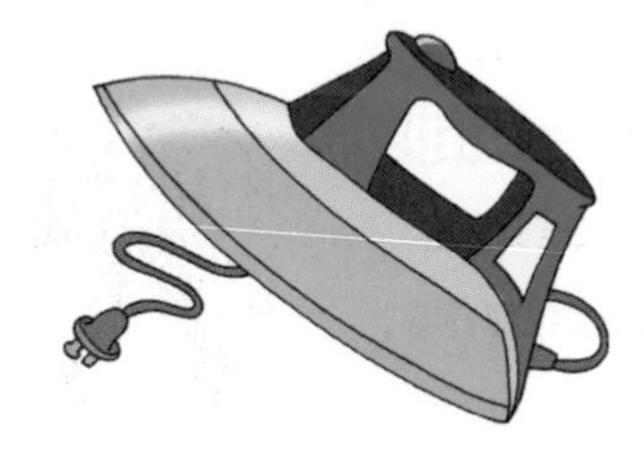

a tool used to press the wrinkles out of your clothes. The **iron** is on and burning hot but the handle stays cool.

---

**island**

a piece of land with water all around it. Three sailors, marooned on an **island**, were finally rescued by a passing ship.

---

**ivy**

a climbing plant with shiny, pointed leaves. The **ivy** has grown up the wall and across the window sill. **Ivy** is an evergreen plant.

# Jj
# Kk

**jaws** the two hinged bones that hold the teeth. A shark has **jaws** with double rows of saw-like teeth.

---

**jelly**

a sweet, shiny, slippery, soft food. The red **jelly** has a strawberry flavor. You eat a bowl of **jelly** with a spoon.

---

**jug** a container for liquids with a handle for pouring. Ken buys a **jug** of juice at the store. Juice **jugs** are made of plastic.

---

**kangaroo**

an Australian animal that jumps. A female **kangaroo** has a pouch in which to carry her baby.

---

**kettle** a container with a handle, lid and spout. Polly puts a **kettle** of water on the stove. The **kettle** whistles when the water boils.

---

**kite**

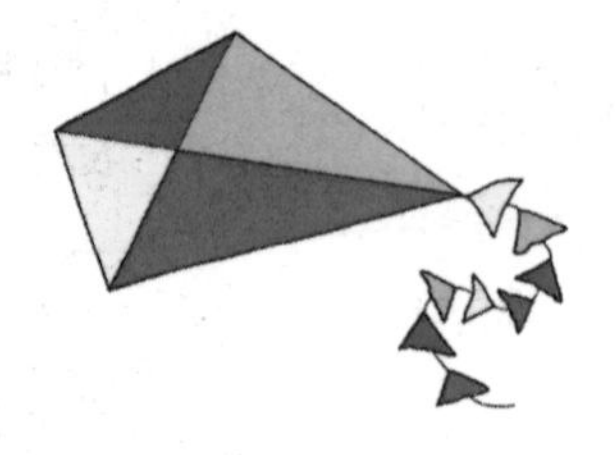

a toy with a long string attatched that you can fly in the wind. I build a **kite** with light wood, tissue paper, string and glue.

---

**koala** a furry, wild animal living in Australia. The **koala**, sitting in the eucalyptus tree, has a baby in her pouch.

**lace**

a piece of string used to tie up shoes and boots. There is a knot in the **lace** of my shoe. Boot **laces** are extra long.

---

**ladder**

a set of steps between two long bars, for climbing up and down. You need a **ladder** to reach the topmost shelf.

---

**lamp**

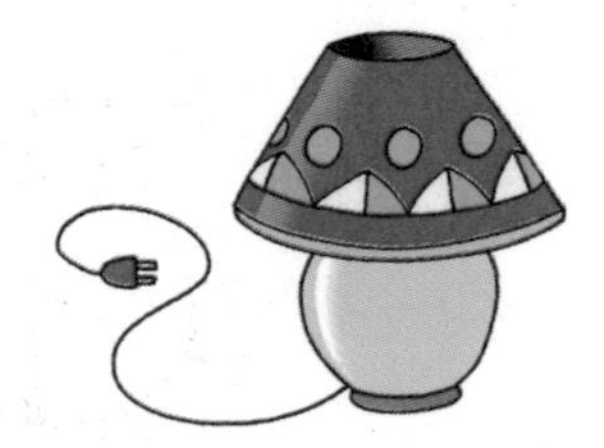

Something that gives light where and when you want it. I turn on my bedside **lamp** to read in bed at night.

---

**laundry**

dirty clothes that need to be washed, or, a place to wash dirty clothes. A washing machine does the **laundry**.

---

**leaf**

one of the flat, green parts of a plant or tree. A maple **leaf** turns red in the fall. One **leaf**, then many **leaves** fall.

---

**leggings**

close-fitting pants made of stretchy material. Jill likes to wear **leggings**. **Leggings** warm up a dancer's legs.

---

**lemon**

a yellow fruit with a very sour taste. **Lemons** have a thick skin. A **lemon** is yellow both inside and out.

# Ll

**lettuce** a green, leafy vegetable. **Lettuce** is eaten raw in salads and sandwiches. My pet rabbit eats **lettuce** everyday.

---

**lilac**

a small tree with sweet-smelling flowers. Our **lilac** has purple flowers that grow in clusters. The smell of **lilacs** fills the air.

---

**lion** a large wild cat found in Africa and India. The male **lion** has a mane. The female **lion**, or *lioness*, hunts for food.

---

**lizard**

a small reptile with four legs and a tail. The sun warms a **lizard**'s body. A **lizard** has a scaly, snakelike skin.

---

**lobster** a sea creature with a shell, two claws, eight legs and a fan-shaped tail. A **lobster** can live to be 70 years old!

---

**lock**

A fastening for a door, gate or box that opens with a key. Just turn the key in the **lock** to open the door.

---

**locomotive** the engine that pulls a train. This old steam **locomotive** is now in a museum.

# Mm

**magnet**

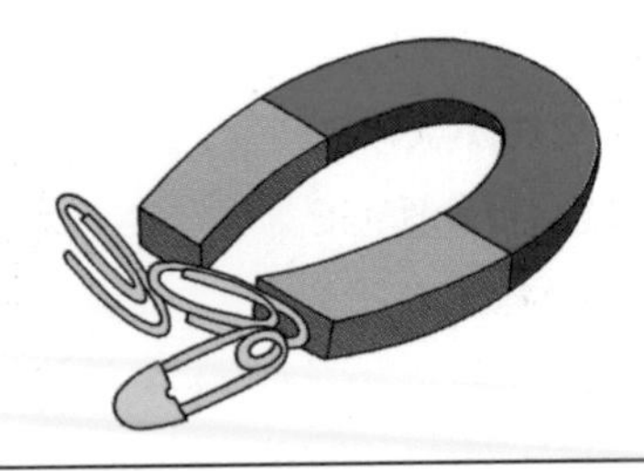

a metal bar that can make pieces of iron and steel stick to it. My toy **magnet** attracts nails and pins.

---

**mammoth**

an extinct animal that looked like a hairy elephant with very long tusks. The **mammoth** no longer exists.

---

**mask**

a cover worn over the face to hide or protect it. Take off that devil's **mask**, then I can see who you are.

---

**medal**

a special reward given for bravery or excellence. Every athlete has dreams of winning a gold **medal**.

---

**mermaid**

in stories, a sea creature that is half woman, half fish. Instead of legs, a **mermaid** has a fish's tail.

---

**milk**

a white, nourishing liquid that mothers and other female mammals feed their babies. We buy cow's **milk** at the dairy.

---

**mirror**

a special kind of glass in which you can see yourself. You need light to see things reflected in a **mirror**.

# Mm

**mitten** a covering for the hand with one part for the thumb and another for the fingers. I lost my other **mitten**.

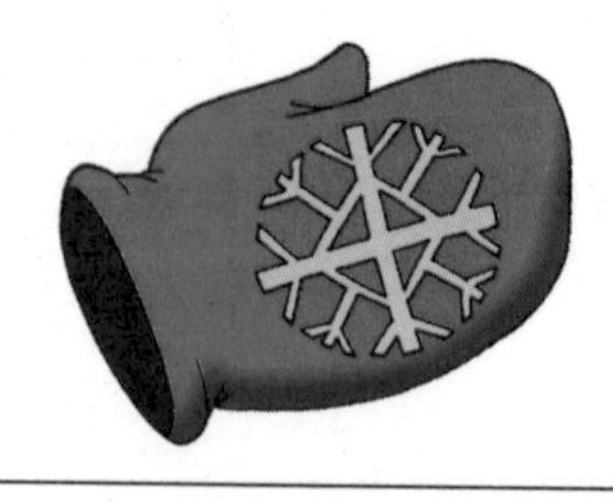

**monkey**

a tropical, tree-climbing animal with long arms and a tail. A **monkey** can swing by its hands and its feet.

**moon** a natural satellite that goes around a planet. Planet Earth has one **moon**. A full **moon** is shining tonight.

**mosaic**

a picture made from colored pieces of paper, glass or stone. A splendid **mosaic** decorates the hotel lobby.

**mountain** land that rises very high. Everest is the world's highest **mountain**. Clouds hide the **mountain** tops.

**mouse**

a small furry animal with a long tail and pointed nose. A female **mouse** will soon have many baby **mice**.

**moustache** hair that grows above a man's upper lip. The barber curls the ends of the man's **moustache**.

**name**

what a person, place or thing is called. What is the **name** of the book you are reading? Mars is the **name** of a planet.

---

**napkin**

a piece of cloth or paper for wiping your lips and fingers at meals. I put a **napkin** beside each dinner plate.

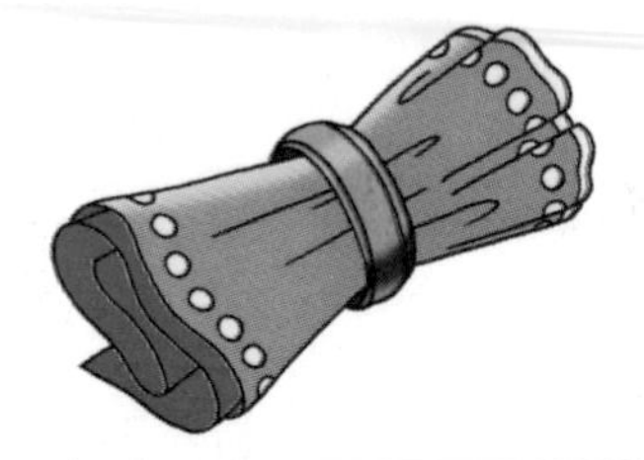

---

**neck**

the body part that attaches the head to the rest of the body. Carol wears a red bandana around her **neck**.

---

**necklace**

a piece of jewelry worn around the neck. The gold **necklace** on the velvet stand is set with a red ruby.

---

**needle**

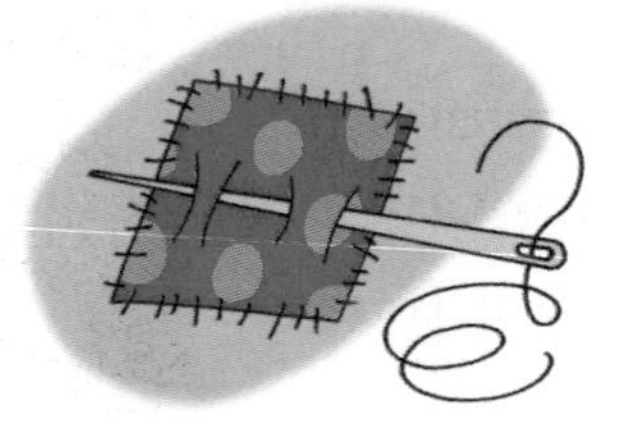

a thin, sharp, pointed piece of metal used for sewing. There is a hole in the **needle** to carry the thread.

---

**nest**

a safe place for their young, made by birds and some other animals. Two birds build a **nest** in our tree.

---

**night**

the time when it is dark. **Night** falls between sunset and sunrise. The moon and the stars shine at **night**.

# Nn

**nightmare** a frightening dream. I woke up from my **nightmare** just as the monster was about to grab me.

---

**nose**

the part of your face that you use for breathing and smelling. Jack's eyes cross when he tries to see his **nose**.

---

**notebook** a small book for writing things down, in case we forget. I write the new words in my **notebook**.

---

**number**

a word or figure that shows how many. They live in unit **number** 73 in an apartment building with 100 units.

---

**nurse** a person trained to look after your health. A **nurse** prepares a needle and gives the patient his flu shot.

---

**nursery rhyme**

a short poem or song for young children. The tale of Humpty Dumpty is a **nursery rhyme**.

---

**nut** a kind of fruit with a hard shell and a softer part inside. Ripe **nuts** fall off the *hazel***nut** tree.

**ocean**

one of the large seas surrounding the land masses of the earth. On a world map, the **oceans** are shown in blue.

---

**octopus**

a sea creature with a soft body and eight long arms with suckers. The **octopus** grabs food with its arms.

---

**omelette**

a food made of eggs beaten together and fried. The **omelette** in the frying pan looks and smells delicious.

---

**orange**

a round, juicy fruit with a thick, yellow-red skin. Inside and out, an **orange** is a yellow-red color called **orange**.

---

**overalls**

a pair of pants with shoulder straps and a bib. A child can crawl with ease wearing a pair of **overalls**.

---

**owl**

a bird that hunts smaller animals at night. An **owl** has big, round eyes, a hooked beak and sharp claws.

---

**oyster**

a soft-bodied, sea creature living inside two shells. Sometimes an **oyster** will produce a pearl.

# Pp

**pail** an open container with a handle. He washes his car with a sponge and a **pail** of soapy water.

---

**paintbox**

a box containing a tray of dry, watercolor paints. There are eight colors in my **paintbox**.

---

**panda** a large animal with white and black fur, found in China. The **panda** looks like a bear with the masked eyes of a raccoon.

---

**parcel**

something wrapped up and ready to be carried or sent away. A mail truck delivers a **parcel** with my name on it.

---

**parrot** a brightly colored tropical bird with a hooked beak that can mimic human speech. This **parrot** talks too much.

---

**pattern**

a repeated design on something. This clay jar is decorated with a **pattern** of circles and wavy lines.

---

**pear** a green or yellow fruit that is narrow at the top and round at the bottom. A ripe **pear** tastes juicy and sweet.

**pencil**

a tool for writing and drawing. You can sharpen a wooden **pencil**. I need some paper and colored **pencils** to draw.

---

**penguin**

a black and white sea bird that cannot fly. A **penguin** uses its short, stiff wings for swimming.

---

**pet**

a tame animal that you keep at home. This is Felix, a happy, chubby, golden hamster and a very pampered **pet**.

---

**piano**

a large musical instrument with a row of black and white keys. You play a **piano** by pressing the keys with your fingers.

---

**pie**

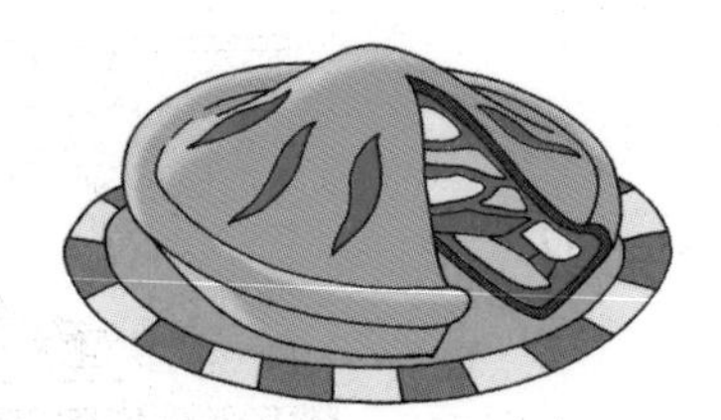

a dish of fruit or meat covered with pastry and baked in the oven. This apple **pie** is flavored with cinnamon.

---

**pillow**

a cushion, on a bed, where you rest your head. She falls asleep as soon as her head touches the **pillow**.

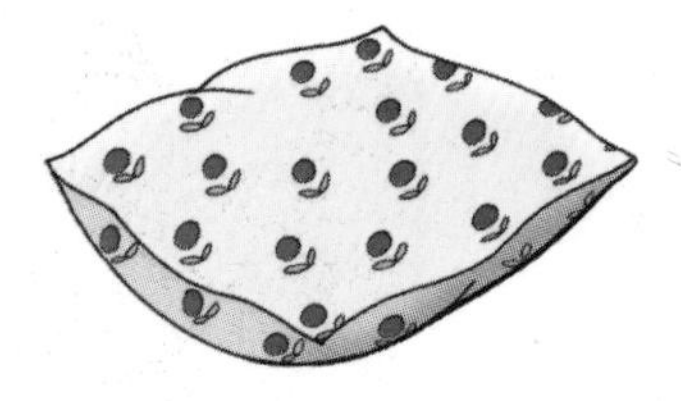

---

**pirate**

a person who once roamed the seas robbing ships. A famous storybook villain is the **pirate**, Captain Hook.

# Pp

**planet** any of the worlds in space that move around a sun. Earth is a **planet** with one moon. **Planet** Saturn has rings.

---

**plate**

a flat, round dish for food. The **plates** are kept in the kitchen cupboard. He left two slices of cheese on his **plate**.

---

**poster** a notice or picture that hangs on a wall. You can put up a **poster** with tacks or tape. Travel **posters** decorate one wall.

---

**potato**

a vegetable that grows underground. Mike peels one **potato** after another. Eight **potatoes** are boiling in the pot.

---

**price** the amount of money it costs to buy something. I cannot afford to buy this dress, the **price** is too high.

---

**prize**

a reward for winning a contest. The jockey and his horse crossed the finish line first and won the gold cup **prize**.

---

**pumpkin** a very large, hard-skinned, orange fruit that grows on the ground. The carved **pumpkin** grins in the dark.

# Pp Qq

**puppy** a very young dog. Both **puppies** are wide awake, but only one **puppy** wants to go for a walk.

**purse**

a handbag, or a small bag just for carrying money. She never leaves home without money in her **purse**.

**puzzle** a game or question that makes you think a lot. A jigsaw **puzzle** is put together piece by piece.

**quarter**

one of four equal parts of something. When four friends share one pizza, each gets a **quarter** of the pie.

**queen** the female ruler of a country, or the wife of a king. The **queen** sits on her throne wearing a crown.

**question**

something you ask when you need an answer. Jerry has a **question**: “Jill, how tall am I?”

**quilt** a bedcover that is filled with padding and stitched in patterns. A **quilt** of colored squares covers the bed.

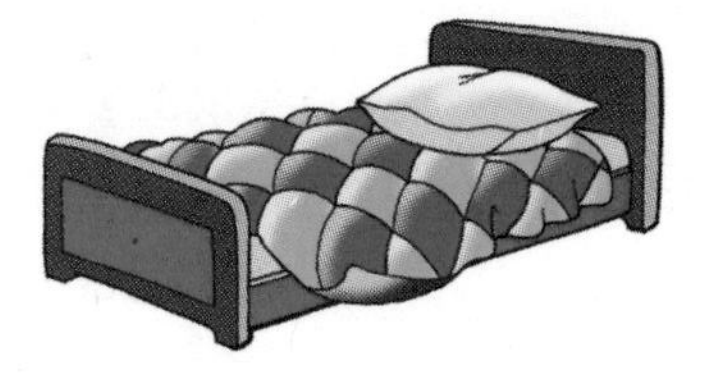

# Rr

**raccoon** a furry, North American animal with masked eyes and a ringed tail. The **raccoon** is active mostly at night.

---

**radio**

an instrument that receives sound signals that we hear as music and words. You listen to the **radio**.

---

**rainbow** an arch of colors, usually in the sky. A **rainbow** appears when the sun shines through rain or mist.

---

**refrigerator**

an electrical machine that keeps food and drinks cold and fresh. The freezer section of a **refrigerator** is extra cold.

---

**reptile** a cold-blooded animal that creeps or crawls and lays eggs. Snakes, turtles, lizards and crocodiles are all **reptiles**.

---

**ring**

a band of metal worn on the finger. The bride-to-be likes to show off her emerald engagement **ring**.

---

**robot** a machine that can do some of the work that people do. I wish I could rent a **robot** to clean up my room.

# Rr

**rocket**

an engine used to push a spacecraft up into space. The **rocket** fires, hot gases rush out, and up, up it goes!

---

**roof**

the covering on top of a building or vehicle. The **roof** is the cover that keeps out the wind and rain.

---

**rooster**

a fully grown, male chicken. Hens and **roosters** are farmyard birds. The **rooster** crows at daybreak.

---

**root**

the part of a plant that grows under the ground. A plant draws food and water from the soil through its **roots**.

---

**rose**

a sweet-smelling flower with thorns on its stem. The gardener plucked a red **rose** and gave it to his sweetheart.

---

**rug**

a piece of thick material used to cover part of a floor. **Rugs** are woven on looms. Let's make believe that this **rug** is a flying carpet.

---

**ruler**

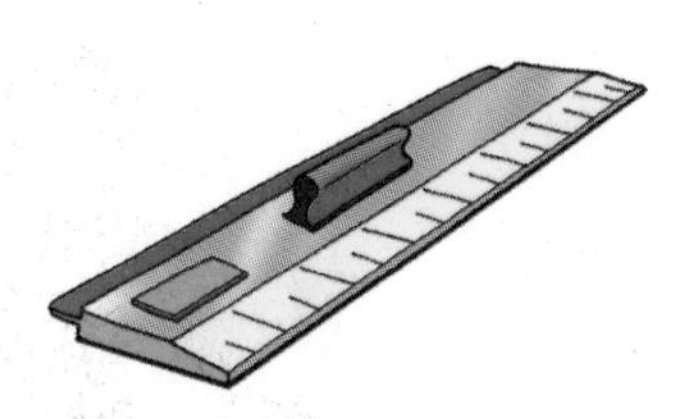

a strip of wood, metal or plastic used to measure things or draw straight lines. I measure my foot with a 12 inch **ruler**.

# Ss

**sail** a sheet of strong cloth attached to a boat. The wind, blowing into the **sail**, makes the boat move.

---

**salad**

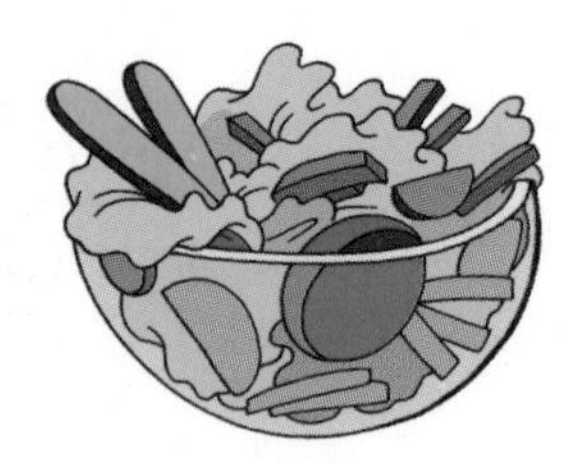

a mixture of cold, raw vegetables or fruits. There is lettuce, tomato and cucumber in this **salad.**

---

**sandal** a light, open shoe with straps to attach it to your foot. I wear my summer **sandals** without socks.

---

**sandwich**

two slices of bread with other food in between. He orders a tomato and cheese **sandwich**.

---

**scales** an instrument for weighing people or things. Six big apples weigh 3 pounds on the grocer's **scales**.

---

**scarf**

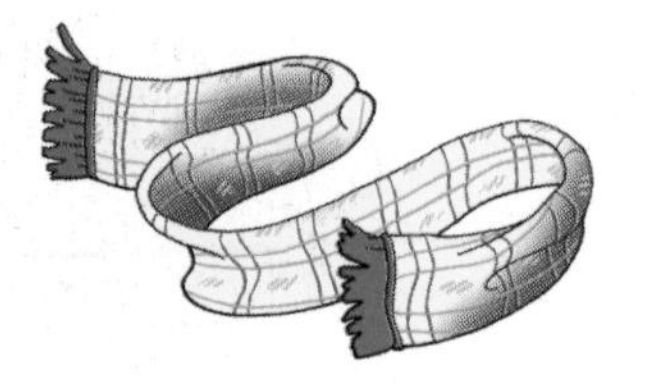

a piece of material worn, for warmth or decoration, around the neck. She knits one long **scarf** and two short **scarves**.

---

**school** a place where children go to be taught. They teach us reading, writing and arithmetic at **school**.

**scissors**

a cutting tool with two blades joined together at the handles. I use a pair of **scissors** to cut paper and cloth.

---

**seashell**

the hard covering that shelters a soft-bodied sea creature. I found an empty **seashell** on the beach.

---

**shadow**

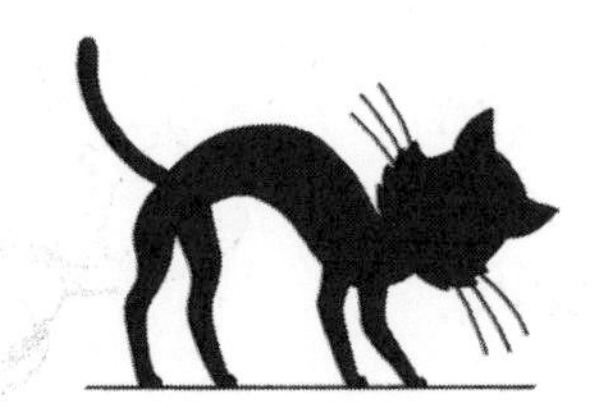

a dark shape caused by something blocking the light. An angry cat is casting a **shadow** on the wall.

---

**shampoo**

a liquid soap for washing your hair. This **shampoo** makes a lot of bubbles without stinging my eyes.

---

**shirt**

a piece of clothing to wear with pants or a shirt. A **shirt** has a collar, sleeves and a row of buttons down the front.

---

**shoe**

a covering for your foot with a stiff sole and heel. You cannot wear your left **shoe** on your right foot.

---

**sink**

a basin with water taps and a drain. You use soap and water to wash your hands in the bathroom **sink**.

# Ss

**skeleton** a framework of bones inside a body. A dinosaur **skeleton** is assembled bone by bone.

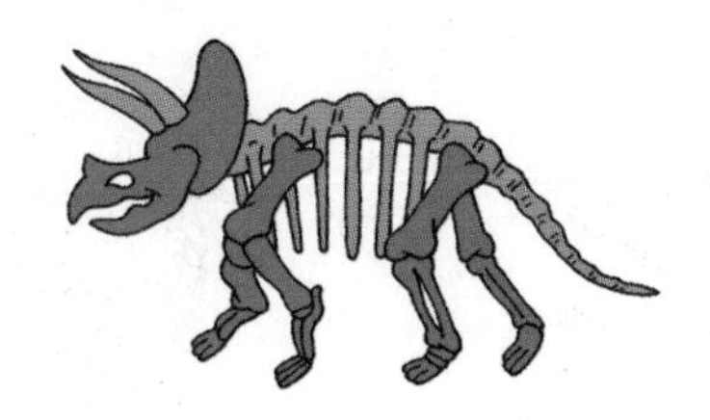

---

**skirt**

a piece of clothing for women and girls, worn around the waist. The **skirt** she is wearing comes down to her knees.

---

**sled** a small vehicle with runners instead of wheels, for traveling over snow. The **sled** speeds down the icy hill.

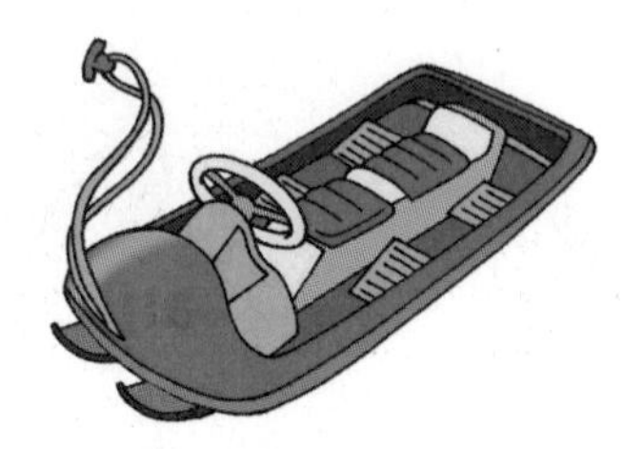

---

**slide**

a playground structure with a ladder to the top for sliding down the other side. The new park **slide** is smooth and fast.

---

**snail** a small, soft-bodied creature that lives inside a shell. **Snails** move slowly. A **snail** travels with its shell on its back.

---

**snout**

an animal's nose and mouth jutting out from the rest of its face. Pigs and dogs have **snouts**. The bear rubs his **snout**.

---

**snow** flakes of frozen water that fall from the sky. In winter you roll the **snow** into three big balls and build a **snow***man*.

**sock** a covering for your foot that you wear inside your shoe. Two **socks** make a pair. The matching **sock** is missing.

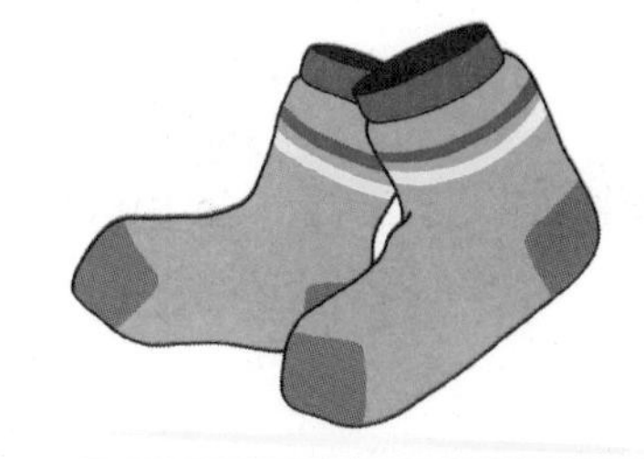

---

**sofa**

a long, comfortable seat with padded arms and back. The **sofa** in the living room seats two big people.

---

**spider** a small creature with eight legs that spins webs. A **spider** eats insects and weaves a web to catch them.

---

**stove**

an appliance for heating a room or for cooking. This electric, kitchen **stove** has four cooking rings and an oven.

---

**suitcase** a kind of box with a handle to put your clothes in for a trip. Gregory boards the train with his **suitcase**.

---

**sun**

any star in the universe with or without planets orbiting around it. Earth gets warmth and light from a distant **sun**.

---

**sweat** the drops of water that come out of your skin when you are hot. Jim stops running to wipe the **sweat** off his face.

# Tt

**table** a piece of furniture with a flat top set on legs. We eat at the kitchen **table**. The wooden **table** has four legs.

---

**taxi**

a car with a driver that you can hire for a short trip. They left the car at home and took a **taxi** to the airport.

---

**teddybear** a stuffed toy that looks like a bear. The child hugs his **teddybear** and falls asleep.

---

**teeth**

more than one tooth. You chew your food with your **teeth**. The baby has grown her first **teeth**.

---

**telephone** an instrument that lets you talk to someone in another place. We talk for hours on the **telephone**.

---

**television**

a special piece of equipment with a screen that shows moving pictures. We all watch **television**.

---

**tiger** a large, wild cat with a striped coat found in India and China. The **tiger** is a fierce hunter of other animals.

**tourist**

a person on holiday who travels around to see places. A **tourist** always has her camera ready.

---

**tower**

a tall, narrow building or a tall part of a building. There is a television **tower** on top of the office **tower**.

---

**toy**

something that a child likes to play with. A rag doll is a **toy**. A wind-up clown and a spinning top are **toys** that move.

---

**tree**

a big, tall plant with one thick stem of wood and many branches. The trunk of a **tree** supports a heavy crown of leaves.

---

**tricycle**

a cycle with three wheels. You ride a **tricycle** on the sidewalk, but a two-wheeled bicycle on the road.

---

**truck**

a road vehicle for hauling heavy loads. Everyday you see all kinds of **trucks** on the road. This **truck** hauls cement.

---

**turtle**

a slow-moving animal with a shell over its body. A **turtle** can pull its head and legs back into its shell.

# Uu

**UFO** a short way of writing Unidentified Flying Object. Some say that the comet we saw was really a **UFO**.

---

**umbrella**

an object you hold over your head to keep you dry in the rain. I open my **umbrella** when it starts to rain.

---

**umpire** a person who makes sure that a game is played by the rules. An **umpire** blew his whistle to stop the hockey game.

---

**underwear**

clothes worn next to the skin under your other clothes. His **underwear** is made of cotton.

---

**unicorn** an imaginary animal with one horn that looks like a horse. A **unicorn** has one long horn in the middle of its forehead.

---

**uniform**

a set of clothes worn by members of a group or team. Our football team has a new **uniform**. Police wear **uniforms**.

---

**universe** everything, everywhere that exists—all energy, matter and space. Astronomers probe the **universe** with big telescopes.

**valentine**

the card given - or the person given the card - on St. Valentine's Day. Al gives Allison a **valentine** and candy.

---

**vase**

a pretty jar for holding flowers. Cut flowers stay fresh in a **vase** full of water. The **vase** is made of glass.

---

**vegetable**

a plant, or its parts, that we eat. Carrots, lettuce, tomatoes, corn, and turnips are all **vegetables**.

---

**vehicle**

anything that takes people or goods from place to place on land. Trucks, cars, buses and bicycles are **vehicles**.

---

**villain**

a person who does bad things. The movie **villain** robs a bank and shoots his way out of town.

---

**violin**

a musical instrument with strings and a bow to play it. Alice tucks the **violin** under her chin and starts to play.

---

**volcano**

a mountain that can spew out fire, hot rock, ash and gas. The **volcano** on Lava Island suddenly erupted.

# Ww

**wagon** a four-wheeled cart with a long handle to pull it along. He uses a **wagon** to deliver newspapers.

---

**wallet**

a small, flat case for carrying money. I keep my **wallet** in my hip pocket. I open my **wallet** to pay for the tickets.

---

**wasp** a flying insect that can sting you. A **wasp** has a yellow body with black stripes, a tiny waist and two wings.

---

**watch**

a small instrument, worn on the wrist, that tells time. My **watch** says it is 10 minutes after 10 o'clock.

---

**waterfall** a stream of water falling from a high to a low place. A **waterfall** plunges down the steep cliff.

---

**whale**

the world's largest sea animal. **Whales** are mammals. A baby **whale** drinks its mother's milk.

---

**wheel** a circle of wood or metal that spins around a fixed rod in its center. The wagon **wheels** are stuck in the mud.

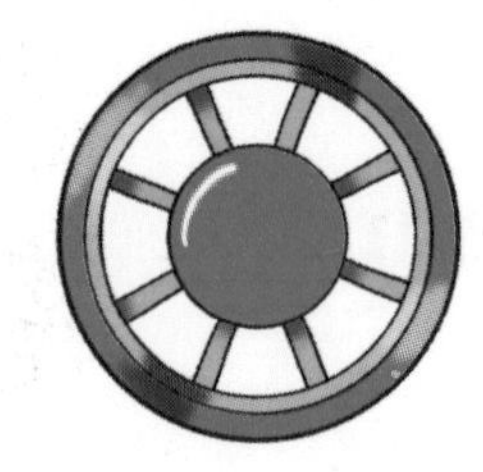

**wig**

a cap of false hair. The hairdresser is styling a lady's **wig**. The nobility of ancient Egypt wore blue **wigs.**

---

**window**

a glass-covered opening in a wall. A **window** serves to let in light. An open **window** lets in fresh air.

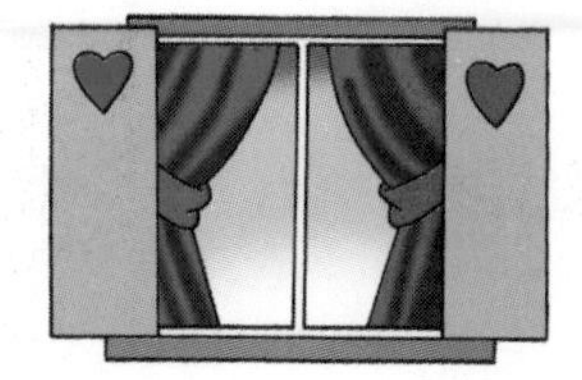

---

**witch**

a woman with supposed magic powers. In stories **witches** do bad things. I can draw a **witch** flying on a broomstick.

---

**wizard**

a man with supposed magic powers. In stories **wizards** are bad and good. A **wizard** has a book of magic spells.

---

**wood**

the stuff of which a tree and its branches are made. She puts more **wood** on the fire. A carpenter makes things from **wood**.

---

**wool**

the soft hair of a sheep, or the thread and cloth made from that hair. There are balls of **wool** in the knitting basket.

---

**wreath**

a ring of leaves or flowers. She twists the flowers into a **wreath** for her head. Christmas **wreaths** are made of holly.

# Xx Yy Zz

**X-ray** a special photograph of the inside of your body. An **X-ray** shows if any bones are cracked or broken.

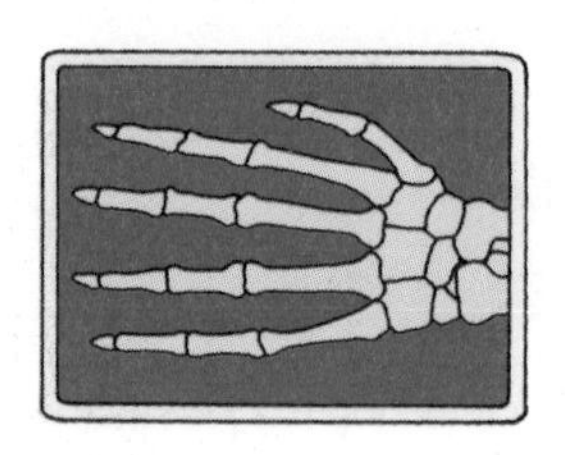

---

**xylophone**

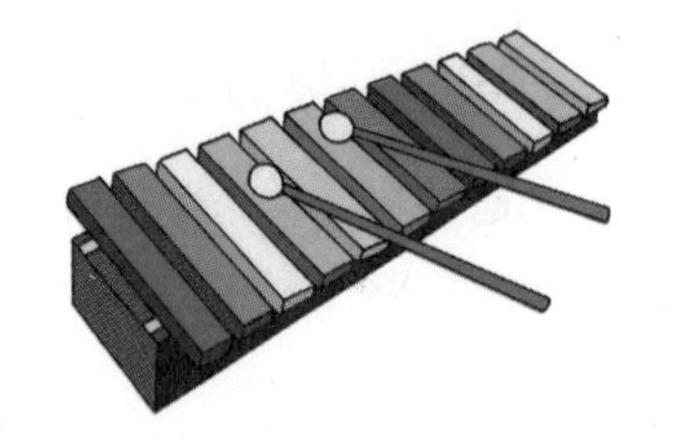

a musical instrument with a row of bars that you strike with soft hammers. I have a toy **xylophone**.

---

**yoghurt** a soft food made from soured milk. You eat **yoghurt** like pudding, with a spoon. I like strawberry **yoghurt**.

---

**yolk**

the round, yellow part inside an egg. A hard-boiled egg has a solid **yolk**. The **yolk** of a poached egg is liquid.

---

**zebra** an animal like a horse with black and white stripes. **Zebras** live in herds in central Africa.

---

**zipper**

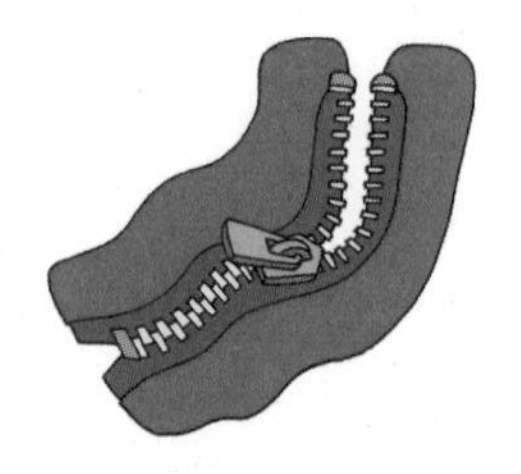

a kind of fastener sewn into clothes, boots and bags. My jacket **zipper** is stuck; I cannot pull it up or down.

---

**zoo** a park for wild animals that you can visit. At the **zoo** the lions of Africa are a short walk away from the Arctic polar bears.